The Den That Octopus Built

Randi Sonenshine

illustrated by
Anne Hunter

CANDLEWICK PRESS

*T*his is the ledge of sandstone and lime,

layered with shells cemented by time,

that shelters the den that Octopus built.

This is the rubble

she siphons and funnels,

cleverly clearing the way as she tunnels

to widen the den that Octopus built.

This is the garden that blooms in her yard

with blossoms of shells and shiny glass shards

in front of the den that Octopus built.

These are her snaky, sucker-lined limbs,
sniffing and probing for prey while she swims
close to the den that Octopus built.

These are the shells she wears like a sheath,

keeping her safe from Tiger Shark's teeth

when she's far from the den that Octopus built.

This is the algae with unblinking eyes,

or is it a cephalopod in disguise

swaying near the den that Octopus built?

This is her capture-the-crab technique:

she pounces, then stabs with her parrot-like beak,

then feasts in the den that Octopus built.

This is the sleek, whiskery seal

seeking a many-armed afternoon meal

above the den that Octopus built.

This is the stream of blinding black ink

she shoots at the seal, then she's gone in a blink,

back to the den that Octopus built.

This is the stone, a strong clever door,

concealing a crevice close to the shore:

the nursery den that Octopus built.

These are the eggs she nurtures with care

with strokes of her suckers and currents of air

clustered in the den that Octopus built.

This is her last breath setting them free,
blowing them out to the wide, waiting sea
away from the den that Octopus built.

This is the one little hatchling alive.

Adrift near the surface, she fights to survive

outside of the den that Octopus built.

This is her down on the seafloor alone,

seeking a rock ledge or reef of her own

to shelter the den that Octopus built.

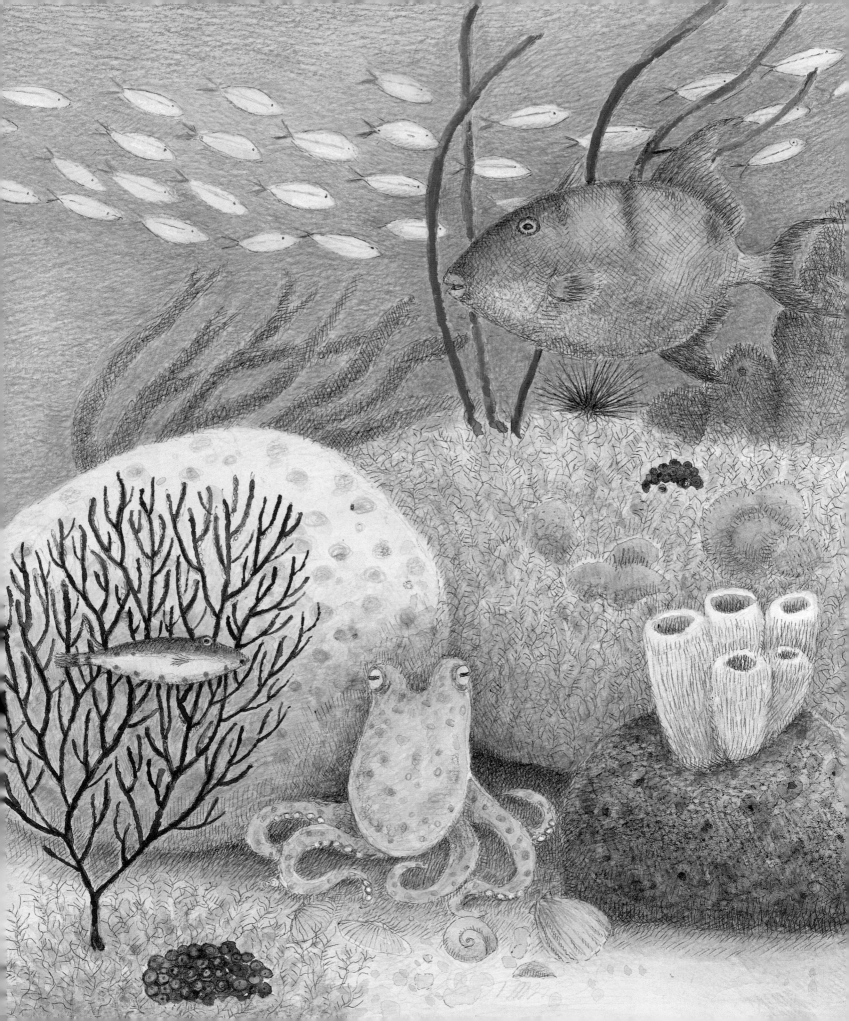

Arm Yourself with Octo-Knowledge

Cephalopod Superstars

What has nine brains, eight arms, three hearts, and blue blood and is older than the dinosaurs? Nope, it's not a new comic book character; it's an octopus! Octopuses have been captivating the interest and imaginations of humans for centuries, and the more scientists study them, the more they realize there is to learn.

Wait! Did You Just Say *Octopuses*?

Although many people mistakenly use the word *octopi* for the plural of *octopus*, if you want to be octo-right, use the word that scientists and word authorities prefer: *octopuses*. Also, octopus limbs are not *tentacles*. Squids have tentacles, which are long and stringy, with suckers only on their clubbed ends, while octopus *arms* are shorter and muscular, with rows of suckers all along their length. Still, you probably wouldn't want to get in a wrestling match with either one!

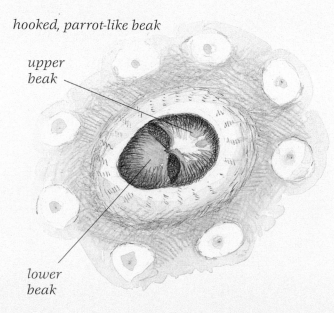

hooked, parrot-like beak

upper beak

lower beak

Octo-Engineering

When they are not hunting, octopuses hide away in dens, moving every few weeks. Dens may be simple hollows in rock beds or coral reefs or elaborate constructions under ledges. First, like eight-armed bulldozers, octopuses may excavate construction sites, clearing away algae, shell fragments, and other debris. Then they may barricade their dens with shells, bottles, or cans or even wedge large rocks in the entrance, to act as doors. Scattered shells, remains of their meals, are often found outside their dens. However, these midden piles, sometimes known as octopus gardens, may also feature sea glass shards, bottle caps, or other trinkets they've collected.

A Wise Old Tale

Octopuses are known for their extraordinary intelligence. They can build dens, solve complex problems, use tools, remember people, and even play! How did the octopus get so smart? That's a story that has been evolving for more than 300 million years. Somewhere along their evolutionary journey, octopuses lost their shells, which left their soft, squishy bodies vulnerable to many predators. To survive, they needed to outswim and outsmart their hunters, so over time, they developed big, beautiful brains and many other octo-spectacular defenses.

Well-Armed Brainiacs

Einstein had only one brain, but an octopus has nine! The large, doughnut-shaped central brain in its head contains only about a third of the 500 million neurons that make up its central

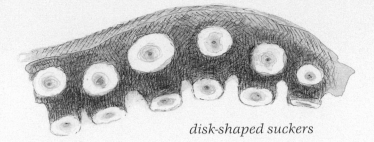

disk-shaped suckers

nervous system. The rest of its neurons, which communicate information between the brain and body, are in its arms, allowing each to act independently. Four arms could be sniffing out prey, two could be prying open a clam, and the other two could be strolling along the seafloor. Talk about multitasking!

Super-Powered Suckers

Imagine if you could smell and taste new food with your fingertips before taking a bite. An octopus can do exactly that! Each of its disk-shaped suckers is loaded with special chemical-detecting receptor cells. With more than 200 suckers on each arm, this sticky cephalopod can learn very quickly about its environment. Each sucker is also incredibly strong—some able to hold up to 35 pounds (16 kilograms)—and nimble enough to pry open stubborn oyster shells. It's no wonder scientists are studying these super-suckers to develop new technology. Promising inventions include medical patches that adhere better to moist tissue, and "sticky robots" that could aid in surgeries.

Masters of Defense

Along with uncanny intelligence and strong, sucker-lined arms, octopuses have developed many features that help them survive. Imagine this scenario: hunting far from its den, with no hiding places in sight, an octopus encounters a fierce predator, the moray eel. It could suction shells around its body like armor, but there are none nearby. Quickly, it fires a cloud of toxic ink at the eel. While its hungry enemy is clouded in confusion, the octopus blasts off with jet propulsion, then vanishes! In less than a second, the octopus has used its remarkable powers of camouflage to change its skin color and texture to blend in with a cluster of coral. The hunt is not over, though. The eel sniffs out its prey and attacks! In an epic battle, the octopus finally wriggles out of the eel's grip and jets away, losing part of an arm in the struggle. The arm will grow back, and this super-powered cephalopod will live another day.

A Short, Not-So-Sweet Life

While a giant Pacific octopus can live as long as five years, most other species live only one or two years. Males die soon after mating, but the female has a very important job to do. After laying anywhere from 100,000 to 500,000 eggs, each the size of a grain of rice, and securing them in strands to the den roof, she guards them for two to eight months (depending on the species). She never leaves the den and obsessively cleans the eggs with currents of oxygenated water from her siphon and strokes of her suckers. When it's time for the eggs to hatch, she blows them out into the ocean, where they drift amid the plankton for several weeks before settling on the seafloor. Unfortunately, there's no happily-ever-after ending for this hardworking mom! She dies a short time later, but with luck, a few of her tiny hatchlings survive to start the cycle all over again.

Glossary

algae: plants or plant-like organisms, such as seaweed, that live in water or moist places

cephalopod: a member of the class of marine animals that includes octopuses, squid, cuttlefish, and nautiluses

crevice: a narrow opening

prey: an animal that is hunted by another for food

probing: examining or exploring closely

reef: a hard ridge found near the surface of the water

rubble: rough bits of hard, solid material such as rock or brick

shards: broken pieces of glass, metal, ceramic, rock, or other hard material

sheath: a protective covering

siphon: a tube-like structure through which water may flow or be propelled; the term may also be used as a verb to describe the action of this structure

Author's Note

There are more than 300 species of octopuses, but the subject of this book is *Octopus vulgaris* (the common octopus). I chose this species because it lives all over the world in many different underwater habitats, so chances are, wherever *you* live, you would find common octopuses in the nearest ocean. The octopus in this book lives in a temperate (not too cold and not too hot) hard-bottom rocky reef, which is different from a tropical coral reef. Hard-bottom reefs can be natural, forming over time from shell fragments and deposits of sand and mud, or they can be artificial, created from human-made materials such as sunken ships, tires, or even subway cars!

Like coral reefs, hard-bottom reefs are very important. They provide a habitat for many kinds of sea plants and animals, support fishing and tourism, and protect our coastlines from storms and erosion. Unfortunately, factors such as global climate change, overfishing, and pollution are harming the health and stability of these beautiful and diverse ecosystems, so it's important to take steps to protect them. One protected reef that provided much inspiration for this book is Gray's Reef, off the coast of Georgia. To explore this beautiful natural marine sanctuary, visit https://graysreef.noaa.gov/.

Acknowledgments

I am deeply indebted to Dr. Daniel Gleason, professor of biology at Georgia Southern University, researcher, and director of the Institute for Coastal Plain Science, for graciously sharing his time, passion, and knowledge of reef ecology and marine invertebrates and for reviewing the text. I also gained valuable insight about octopuses through a close encounter with Rita, the Georgia Aquarium's resident giant Pacific octopus, thanks to senior manager Carly Pope, senior aquarist Zelie Wooten, and assistant manager of Dive Immersion Programming Ben Kappel, who set things in motion.

For my mom and sisters, the best mothers I know

RS

For Richard, who also grew up in the sea

AH